How We Used to Live

Memories of SCHOOL AND PLAYTIME

The boys in this picture are playing leapfrog. This was a popular game for children in the past and is still played today.

By Ruth Owen

Published in 2025 by **Ruby Tuesday Books Ltd.**

Copyright © 2025 **Ruby Tuesday Books Ltd.**

All rights reserved. No part of this publication may be reproduced in whole or in part, stored in any retrieval system, or transmitted in any form or by any means, electronic, mechanical, photocopying, recording, or otherwise, without written permission from the publisher.

Editor: Mark J. Sachner
Design & Production: Emma Randall

Photo credits:
Alamy: 5TL (Roger Bamber), 10B (The Picture Art Collection), 11T (Roger Bamber), 11C (KGPA Ltd), 18 (imagebroker.com), 19 (Allan Cash Picture Library), 20C (Homer Sykes), 21T (Trinity Mirror/Mirrorpix), 22T (Allan Cash Picture Library); istock Photo: 3BR (Benjimen Green), 4R (Tommy Lee Walker), 6R (Tommy Lee Walker), 10T (Shelly Still), 10C (Benjimen Green); Mary Evans Picture Library: 8 (Illustrated London News Ltd), 9T (Peter Higginbotham), 13T, 15T (Robert Hunt Collection), 17T (Roger Mayne Archive); Wolfgang Moroder: 11BL; Public Domain: 11BR, 12T; Ruby Tuesday Books: 4L, 5TR; Shutterstock: Cover (Elena Schweitzer/Charles Taylor/Aldo Risolvo/Mazur Travel/OneLight Studio/Becky Stares), 3TL (Mazur Travel), 3BL (Iunamarina), 3TR (Salman211 Khan), 4R (Becky Stares), 5B (Vasylchenko/Simun Galic), 6L (Mazur Travel/Santi S), 7 (Lili Graphie), 9B (Shaiith), 11BR (Mega Pixel), 12B (Margrit Hirsch/Salman211 Khan/Squeeb Creative/Graeme Dawes), 13C (Rostislav Ageev), 14 (Jake Owen Powell), 15B (Jake Owen Powell), 16 (Vasylchenko/Simun Galic), 17B (Simun Galic), 20R (Sarah2), 20B (Mr Doomits), 21B (Elena Larina), 22B (Iunamarina), 23B (Interfoto); Superstock: Cover & 1 (NMPFT/SSPL/Science and Society), 23T (World History Archive).

British Library Cataloguing in Publication Data (CIP) is available for this title.

ISBN: 978-1-78856-423-6

Printed in Poland by L&C Printing

www.rubytuesdaybooks.com

CONTENTS

Looking into the Past 4

A Victorian Schoolroom 6

Learning a Trade 8

Toys from the 1800s 10

The Farthing Bundle 12

A Wartime Drill 14

Bomb Site Playgrounds 16

Junk Playgrounds 18

Playing Out 20

Toys from the 1900s 22

Glossary, Index, Answers 24

LOOKING INTO THE PAST

In this book, we are going to look at **historical** photographs from the 1800s and 1900s. They capture moments from Britain's **past**.

We will read the real-life **memories** of people who lived through some of the times in the photos.

We will also look at photos of objects that people once owned and used.

Together, photos, memories and objects help us to learn how we used to live.

Look at the photos on these pages. How do you think these objects could be connected to school and play in the past?

(The answers are inside the book or on page 24.)

What Is a Century?

We measure history in periods called **centuries**.
A century lasts for 100 years. Today, we are in the 21st Century.

| **1801 to 1900** | **1901 to 2000** | **2001 to 2100** |
| 19th Century | 20th Century | 21st Century |

Many of the photos in this book are from a time that we call "living history". It's a time that people who are still alive today can remember.

A VICTORIAN SCHOOLROOM

In a **Victorian** schoolroom, the pupils sat in rows at wooden desks.

They were taught reading, writing and arithmetic (maths), such as times tables.

The teacher wrote sentences on the blackboard. Then the pupils practised their handwriting by exactly copying the teacher's words.

Young children wrote on slates with slate pencils. Older children wrote with a fountain pen into paper notebooks called copy books.

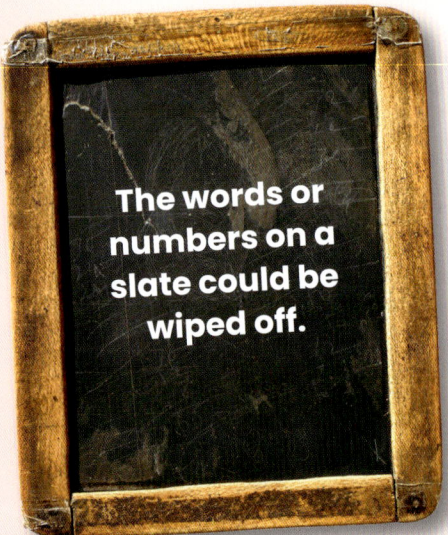

The words or numbers on a slate could be wiped off.

A fountain pen was dipped into ink in an inkwell.

Slate pencil

The inkwell was in the top of the desk.

Fountain pen

A Victorian schoolroom had bare walls.

Teacher

The windows were high, so children could not look out during lessons.

Victorian teachers were very strict. Laziness, talking, rudeness, fidgeting or even scratching yourself was punished! Pupils could be hit on the bottom or hands with a long, thin stick called a cane.

Victorian pupils also had drill, or PE, lessons. Drill included stretching, running on the spot and marching.

During schoolroom lessons, only the teacher talked. The pupils did not work in groups or with a friend. Each child worked alone – in complete silence!

LEARNING A TRADE

During Victorian times, many children lived in terrible poverty.

Some were orphans or had parents in prison. Sometimes parents abandoned a child because they were too poor to raise them.

Some of these children were sent to live at schools known as district schools.

The children did lessons in schoolrooms. But they were also taught a **trade** in the school's workshops, kitchen or laundry room.

Girls learning to wash clothes in a laundry room

Girls were taught housework and cooking. They learned how to wash, iron, mend and make clothes. These skills helped them to get jobs as cooks or maids in the homes of wealthy families.

The schools hoped the children would earn money from their trade and leave behind their lives of poverty.

Boys learning to make shoes in a workshop

Shoemaking equipment

Boys were taught how to grow crops and raise farm animals. They learned carpentry, metalwork, plumbing and shoe-making. Some learned a musical instrument and joined an army band.

TOYS FROM THE 1800s

In the 1800s, only wealthy families could afford to buy toys. Children living in poverty might only have one homemade toy, or no toys at all.

Dominoes made of ivory from elephant tusks

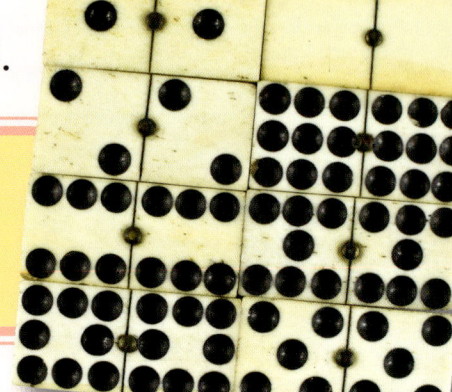

Victorian children played dominoes to help them learn numbers and improve their maths.

A model of a Victorian rocking horse

Ride-on toy horses were first made in the 1600s. They were used to help young, wealthy children learn to ride. Rocking horses became very popular in the 1800s.

Victorian children played with small toy animals carved from wood.

Wooden Noah's Ark

Some families did not want their children to play on Sunday because it was a day for church and prayer. However, a wooden Noah's Ark toy would be allowed because it showed a Bible story.

Victorian clockwork tigers

Key

In the 1800s, toy makers created moving clockwork dolls, animals and trains.

Clockwork toys contained similar parts to the inside of a clock. Children turned a key to wind up the toy and make it move.

Both rich and poor children played rolling a hoop. They used a stick to help keep the hoop rolling for as long as possible.

Hoop

Many children owned a peg doll made from wooden clothes pegs or small pieces of wood.

Young Victorian girls sewed dresses for their dolls from leftover scraps of fabric, lace and ribbon.

Peg doll

Clothes peg

11

THE FARTHING BUNDLE

In the Bow area of London, a head teacher named Clara Ellen Grant wanted to help fight poverty.

In 1907, she set up an action group called the Fern Street Settlement. The group helped local families get food, clothes, medical treatment and toys!

Every weekend, young children queued outside the group's building. If a child was small enough to fit under a wooden archway, they paid a farthing and received a toy bundle.

Boys chose a bundle from the boys' basket and girls chose from the girls' basket.

Clara Ellen Grant

The farthing bundles contained small toys and fun objects such as mini teddy bears, little cars, toy soldiers, marbles, jigsaws, pencils, seashells and beads.

Wooden archway

A queue outside the Fern Street Settlement in the 1930s

Toy bundles wrapped in newspaper

A farthing was a tiny coin that was worth quarter of a penny.

Rupert (Born 1939)

"My dad used to queue up for a Saturday farthing bundle. He said it was a sad day once you got too tall to fit under the arch. Some kids cheated a little and bent their knees. The adult helpers often let them through because they knew the kids had very little at home."

A WARTIME DRILL

In **World War II**, many schools were bombed. If their school was damaged, children might have lessons outdoors, in churches or even in pubs!

One important wartime school activity was the daily gas mask **drill**.

During the war it was feared that the Germans would drop poisonous gas **bombs** on Britain.

The British government gave everyone a protective gas mask to carry with them at all times.

When their teacher shouted, "Gas, gas," children had to practise putting on their masks as quickly as possible.

Straps to hold mask on head

This part contained substances to soak up poisons, so only clean air was breathed in.

Children aged two to five were given colourful gas masks. They were nicknamed "Mickey Mouse masks" to make them sound less scary. Even young children practised putting on their masks.

A school gas mask drill in 1939

During a gas mask drill children had to:

1) Remove the mask from its box.
2) Put the mask onto their face.
3) Check the mask was fitting correctly.
4) Breathe normally.

A gas mask was carried in a cardboard box with a strap that hung over a person's shoulder.

BOMB SITE PLAYGROUNDS

During World War II, German bombing raids destroyed schools, factories, houses and even whole streets.

The empty spaces covered with heaps of rubble and twisted metal were known as bomb sites.

They were dangerous places to go, but they soon became exciting playgrounds for kids.

Children used bricks and pieces of wood to build camps in **derelict** buildings. They played hide-and-seek and war games.

During the war, kids also searched through the rubble hunting for shrapnel.

Shrapnel

Shrapnel is pieces of metal from exploded bombs and shells. In World War II, kids liked to collect shrapnel and swap pieces from their collections with friends.

There were bomb sites in London and other cities for years after World War II.

These children are playing on a bomb site in 1954.

Eddie (Born 1933)

" One night in the war, four houses in the next street were flattened during an air raid. We walked by the wreckage on our way to school the next morning. My older brother picked up a piece of shrapnel that had landed in the street – it was still warm! "

JUNK PLAYGROUNDS

After World War II, some bomb sites became a new kind of place to play – junk, or adventure, playgrounds.

Local councils and action groups wanted places where kids could play outdoors.

Children were allowed to make dens. They collected wood and lit bonfires.

They even built their own climbing frames, slides and swings from scrap materials such as wood, metal, old tyres and ropes.

An adult playworker kept watch. But at junk playgrounds, kids could take **risks** and do their own thing!

In the past, adults often allowed children to do things that could be dangerous. Today, adults try harder to keep children safe as they play.

Since the 1990s, soft safety materials are placed on the ground beneath play equipment. This climbing frame from the 1960s was built on a hard, concrete school playground!

PLAYING OUT

If you ask someone who was a child before the 1980s how they used to play, they will probably remember "playing out".

Children might spend all day with friends in parks or woods without their parents knowing where they were.

Kids played in the streets because there were fewer cars on the roads.

Football, cricket, hide-and-seek, leapfrog, hopscotch, skipping and conkers were all popular games.

Girls playing hopscotch in the 1970s

Hopscotch could be drawn on the street with chalks.

A favourite activity was tying a rope to a streetlight and taking turns to swing around the lamp post!

Kids swinging on a lamp post in 1945

To tie a rope to the top of a lamp post, one child would stand on the shoulders of another and then climb up.

Steve (Born 1955)

"In the summer holidays, we'd go out to play after breakfast. We used to make tunnels and camps in haystacks in the fields behind our house. Once it started to get dark, Mum would bang a wooden spoon in a saucepan and shout at the top of her voice for me to come in!"

Haystack

21

TOYS FROM THE 1900s

In the 1900s, kids played with footballs, board games and even video games. But they looked very different to today.

Children have played with spinning tops for thousands of years. The player tries to keep the top spinning for as long as possible.

A metal spinning top from the 1950s

In the first half of the 1900s, football was played with balls made of leather panels. The panels were stitched together by hand.

A model of a 1940s football

If a game was played in wet weather, a leather football soaked up water. The ball became heavier and heavier, making it painful to head the ball.

In the 1950s, people were starting to understand that robots would be a part of the future. A board game called *The Amazing Magic Robot* was invented.

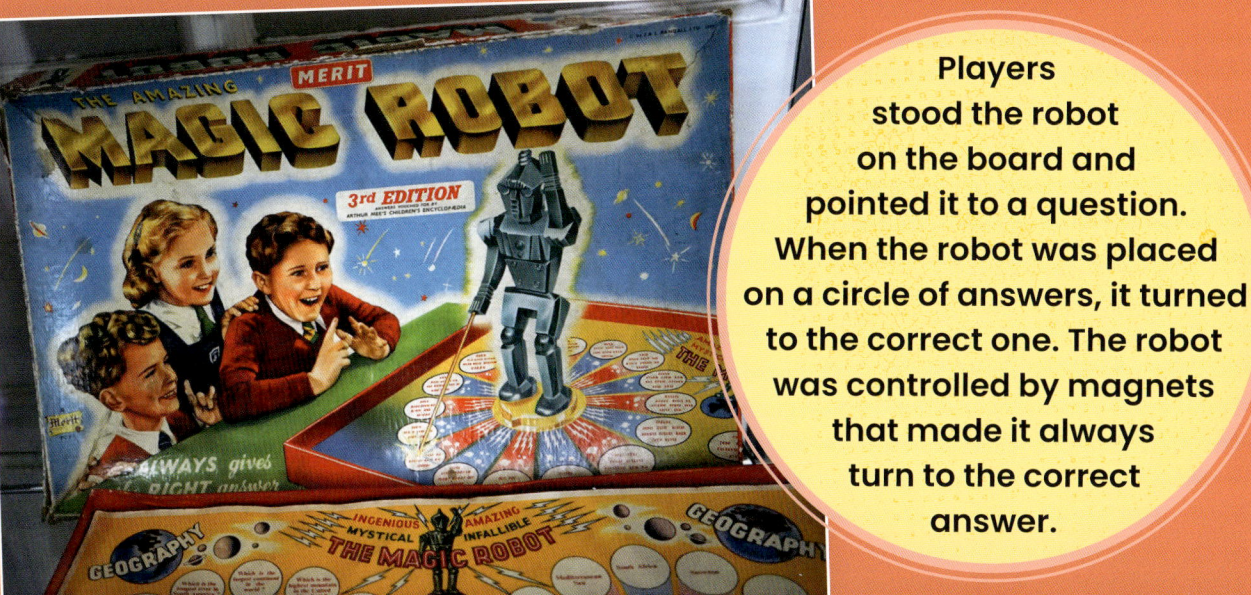

Players stood the robot on the board and pointed it to a question. When the robot was placed on a circle of answers, it turned to the correct one. The robot was controlled by magnets that made it always turn to the correct answer.

Today, there are millions of video games. In the early 1970s, however, very few children played video games – until *Pong*!

An advertisement for *Pong*

Video games could be played on machines in **arcades**. But *Pong* was one of the first that could be played on your TV at home. Just like ping pong, or table tennis, a player tried to get the tiny, square computerised ball past their opponent.

GLOSSARY

arcade
A fun place where people played video games, pinball and other games on coin-operated machines.

bomb
An explosive object that is dropped onto a target.

derelict
Falling down and in a very poor condition.

drill
A regular training exercise to practise a series of actions, such as a fire drill.

historical
From history, or the past.

memory
Something remembered from the past.

past
A time that has already happened.

risk
An action that could be dangerous.

shell
An explosive projectile, such as a torpedo, that can travel towards its target through air or water.

trade
A set of skills that allow a person to earn money – for example, plumbing is a trade.

Victorian
From the years 1837 to 1901 when Queen Victoria reigned.

World War II
A major war that lasted from 1939 to 1945. It was fought between the allies (Britain, France, the United States, the Soviet Union and others) and the Axis powers (Germany, Italy and Japan).

INDEX

B
bomb sites 16–17, 18

C
classrooms (schoolrooms) 4, 6–7, 8–9, 10–11, 14–15

G
games 10–11, 16, 20–21, 22–23
gas masks 14–15

Grant, Clara Ellen 12

J
junk playgrounds 18

P
poverty 8–9, 10–11, 12–13

S
shrapnel 5, 16–17

T
toys 5, 10–11, 12–13, 22–23

V
Victorian schools 6–7, 8–9

W
World War II 14, 16–17, 18

Answers pages 4–5: 1: This item is a model of a pair of Victorian finger stocks. To stop a child fidgeting or even picking their nose in class, their hands were put behind their back. Then their fingers were placed in the stocks and their hands and wrists were tightly tied with the ribbons! **2:** An inkwell in the top of a Victorian wooden school desk, see pages 6–7. **3:** A pair of Victorian wind-up, or clockwork, tigers. When their keys were turned, the tigers walked and growled. **4:** In the early 1900s, some schools did not make school dinners for their pupils. However, children could bring a potato to school to be baked in the school's oven to make a hot lunch. Each child carved their initials into their raw potato. **5:** Pieces of shrapnel, see pages 16–17.